Baking and Cooking in Switzerland:

Famous Swiss Recipes

Lachlan Anderson

Baking and Cooking in Switzerland: Famous Swiss Recipes

Lachlan Anderson

Independently published

ISBN 979-8739172532

Table of Contents

FOREWORD

I am Scottish but I have lived in Switzerland for more than 20 years.

I like to cook and I like to write. Therefore, I have already written two cookbooks. One about typical "Coorie" recipes of Scotland and one about Cooking with Beer (50 Easy Recipes for Cooking with Beer).

Living and cooking in Switzerland has inspired me to put together this cookbook of my discoveries of Swiss recipes. You will find a photo for every recipe as well as some tips or special information about the recipes in many cases.

I hope that you enjoy these meals!

Lachlan

BREAD
&
APPETIZERS

BERNESE BUTTER PLAIT
("Berner Butterzopf")

Ingredients for 1 Zopf

500 g	Flour
1 teaspoon	Sugar
2 Tea spoon	Salt
60 g	Butter
20 g	Yeast
300 ml	Milk
1	Egg

Preparation

Total time about 35 minutes

Put 500 g of flour in a bowl add 1 teaspoon of sugar and 2 teaspoons of salt.

Melt 60 g butter. Dissolve the yeast in the milk and add the melted butter, add the whole mixture to the flour.

Mix the flour with the liquid from the middle. Knead the dough well until it is smooth. Cover and let heat double. Form the dough into two strands of equal length, which are a little thicker in the middle, braid the plates and put them on prepared sheet. Whisk 1 egg, mix the egg yolk with a little water and brush the braid with it.

Bake the braid in the preheated oven at 220 ° C in the lower half of the oven for about 30 minutes.

Special tips:

The Zopf is a typical breakfast bread in Switzerland at weekends.

Experiment with the baking time to experience how dry or wet you like your "Zopf". The baking time is also very depending on your oven.

The Zopf is at its best if you eat it with some butter spread on the slices.

The Zopf also becomes dry rather fast. Better eat it fresh!

SWISS BURLI ("Bürli")

Ingredients for 4 portions

375 g	Flour (wheat flour)
500 g	Water
40 g	Yeast
20 g	Salt
100 g	Dough (wheat sourdough)

Preparation

Total time about 3hours 35 minutes

First, make a wheat sourdough from 50 g wheat flour type 1050, add a crumb of yeast and let it go overnight or very warm. Then put everything together and knead into dough. Then let the dough rise for approx. 30 minutes, weigh into pieces of approx. 60 g and then work round. Now place two pieces together on a well-floured cloth and let it cook. Then bake with steam at approx. 230-240 ° C for approx. 25 minutes. To do this, place a Reindl with water on the bottom of the oven. After 10 minutes let the steam out of the oven and finish baking.

SWISS-STYLE PORRIDGE

Ingredients for 4 portions

200 g	Oatmeal
1 liter	Milk
20 g	Butter
Cinnamon	
Sugar	

Preparation

Total time about 20 minutes

Put the oatmeal, milk and butter in a pan and heat. Stir constantly so that the milk does not burn. Allow to boil for 10 minutes, stirring constantly. Then let it swell for 5 minutes on the switched off hob.

Season to taste with cinnamon and sugar and serve. For this you can pre-mix sugar and cinnamon in a separate small bowl, so that everyone can take only as much as she or he likes.

Special tips:

This is great for breakfast or a small sweet dinner. It could also go under the dessert section of this book ...

SWISS SAUSAGE SALAD ("Schweizer Wurstsalat")

Ingredients for 5 portions

600 g	Lyoner (veal sausage)
1 large	Onion
4 large ones	Pickle Spreewald style, cut into cubes
4 m. In size	Tomatoes
1	Bell pepper, red, marinated from the glass
300 g	Cheese
6 tbsp	Vinegar (salad master wholegrain or old master wine vinegar)
3 splashes	Sweetener or sugar
½ tsp.	Salt
1 teaspoon	Mustard medium hot
1 teaspoon	Pepper, more colorful, from the mill
6 teaspoon	Safflower oil or other neutral oil

| 120 ml | Water, possibly more |
| 1 bunch | Chives, finely chopped |

Preparation

Total time about 1 hour 30 minutes (whereof 1 hour waiting time, optional)

Skin the lyons first slice them, then thin strips. Peel the onion and cut it into thin rings, if necessary, water it a little so that the heat decreases. Drain the pickles and peppers from the glass and cut them into slices, then into small cubes. Wash the tomatoes and cut them into wedges. Also cut the Leerdamer or Emmental cheese into narrow strips.

Put everything together in a large bowl. Baste with the marinade of vinegar, salt, pepper, mustard and sweetener or a little sugar, oil and water and mix everything well.

The sausage salad should soak in the refrigerator for at least an hour, if possible. Season a little if necessary.

Sprinkle with chives before serving.

Fresh farm bread tastes particularly good!

HAM CROISSANTS ("Schinkengipfel")

Ingredients for 4 portions

200 g	Ham, cooked without rind
1	Onion, finely chopped
1 bunch	Parsley, finely chopped
1 teaspoon	Butter
1 teaspoon	Mustard
Salt	
Pepper	
2 teaspoon	Cream
400 g	Puff pastry
1	Egg

Preparation

Total time about 20 minutes

Heat the butter.

Steam the onion and parsley with constant turning for 10 minutes.

Finely chop the ham and put it in a bowl, add the onion and parsley mixture, the mustard, salt, pepper and cream and mix well. Roll out the puff pastry and cut out triangles. Transfer from the filling to the triangles and roll up to the top. The croissants on a lined with baking paper sheet set, with beaten good brush egg yolk and bake in preheated oven at 190 degrees for about 25 minutes until golden brown.

Special tips:

Ham croissants are a great appetizer together with some wine or a beer.

You could serve them with salad for a full meal.

BRAID WITH CREAM

Ingredients for 1 braid

500 g	Flour
½ cube	yeast
1 teaspoon	Sugar
½ teaspoon	Salt
250 ml	Milk
125 ml	Cream
1	Egg

Preparation

Total time about 3 hours 40 minutes

Warm the milk, cream and sugar slightly (but not more than lukewarm, otherwise the yeast will die), remove from the fire, add the yeast and stir until it has melted.

Mix the flour and salt, then add the liquid and knead until the dough is soft and smooth. Place the dough in a bowl, cover with a damp cloth and leave to rise in a warm place for about 2 hours (possibly heat the oven to 50 degrees, switch it off and then put the dough in it).

Then form a nice braid, put it on the baking sheet, brush with the egg and let it rise again in the cold (in the fridge or outside) for about 1 hour.

Then bake in the preheated oven at 220 degrees for about 30-35 minutes and enjoy while still warm!

MILK ROLL ("Milchbrötchen")

Ingredients for about 10 pieces

500 g	Wheat Flour
2 Tea spoons	Salt
½ cube	Yeast or tsp dry yeast
½ tbsp	Baking malt
25 g	Butter, soft
200 ml	Milk and
200 ml	Water, mixed

For painting:

1 cup	Milk with some sugar or
1	Egg yolk, mixed with 2 tablespoons milk

Preparation

Total time about 2 hours 20 minutes

Knead soft yeast dough from all ingredients. Leave for 30 minutes, fold, leave for 30 minutes, fold, and leave for 30 minutes. Divide the dough into about 14 portions and shape them into balls. Press in well with a dough horn in the middle. Let go again about 30 minutes. Then brush with milk and a little sugar or diluted egg yolk.

Bake for 20 to 25 minutes in an oven preheated to 200 ° C. Alternatively, bake the first 5 minutes at 250 ° C

MAIN COURSES

SWISS STYLE PORK FILLETS

Ingredients for 4 portions

200 g	Cheese, Appenzeller, in thick slices
2	Pork fillet (s), each about 400 g
1 teaspoon	Pepper, black from the mill
2 Tea spoons	Paprika powder, hot
1 teaspoon	Dried thyme
1 teaspoon	Oregano, dried
Salt	
2 teaspoon	Clarified butter
125 ml	Meatsoup
200 g	Creme fraiche Cheese
1 bunch	Parsley, smooth
	Lemon juice

Preparation

Total time about 45 minutes

Debark the cheese and cut into about 2 cm long pencils. Cut slits all around in the fillets and press in the cheese sticks.

Mix the pepper with the paprika, thyme, oregano and very little salt and turn the peppered pork fillets into it.

Heat the clarified butter in a roaster and fry the pork fillets all around. Deglaze with the meat broth, stir in the crème fraiche and cover and simmer for about 25 minutes.

Wash the parsley, shake dry, pluck and chop finely. Season the sauce with salt, pepper and lemon juice and finally stir in the parsley.

Serve the sliced fillets.

Narrow ribbon pasta or mashed potatoes with fresh herbs and lettuce are suitable as a side dish.

Tip: The type of cheese can be exchanged as you wish, and various cheese residues are also very suitable for this.

ZURICH SLICED ("Züri Gschnätzlets)

Ingredients for 4 portions

4 teaspoon	Onions, peeled and chopped
160 g	Mushrooms
560 g	Veal cutlet, hand-sliced (3mm thick)
Salt	
Pepper	white from the mill
1 teaspoon	Flour
2 teaspoon	Oil (peanut oil)
3 teaspoon	Butter
200 ml	Wine, white
400 ml	Cream

Preparation

Total time about 30 minutes

Season the sliced meat with salt and pepper from the grinder and divide it into two parts.

Heat a large teflon pan with half of the peanut oil very well, add part of the meat and sauté briefly, not too long, otherwise the meat will become tough and dry

Take the meat out of the pan, keep warm. Do the same with the rest of the meat.

Heat the butter in the same pan, add the onions and stew. Add the sliced mushrooms, dust with the flour and mix. Add white wine and reduce by half. Add the meat juices and the cream and boil everything to the desired consistency season with salt and pepper.

Put the meat in the sauce (do not cook anymore) and mix.

Serve with hash browns or typically Swiss with the following Rösti (next recipe).

RÖSTI

Ingredients for 4 portions

500 g   Potato, firm cooking

4 spoons   Oil (peanut)

Salt and pepper

Butter

Preparation

Total time about 30 minutes (but with pre-cooked and cooled-off potatoes)

Boil the potatoes about 30 minutes. Let them cool. This is best done one or two days before you need the Rösti. At the day you do the Rösti: Peel and grate the potatoes. Season with salt and pepper. Heat oil in a coated frying pan. Spread potatoes loosely and regularly on the bottom of the frying pan. After a few minutes, gently push the potatoes together at the edge with a ladle to create the typical shape. Fry on low heat for approx. 12 minutes. Turn the Rösti in the air (only if you are sure you can do it!) or with the help of a plate. When turning with a plate, brush the plate with a little oil beforehand so that the Rösti slides easily from the plate back into the pan. Be careful not to let the hot oil from the pan drip onto your hands. Fry Rösti for about 10 more minutes until golden brown. Add butter along the edge and fry for about 2 minutes. The butter gives the Rösti the fine aroma. However, it should only be foamed. Serve the Rösti while it is crispy on the outside and steaming hot on the inside.

The Rösti are the perfect and typical side dish for the Zurich Sliced (the previous recipe).

LUCERNE CHEESECAKE ("Luzerner Käsewähe")

Ingredients for 4 portions

400 g	Flour
4 m	Egg
90 g	Butter, cold
1 pinch	Salt
1 pack	Puff pastry
200 g	Ham
200 g	Cheese, grated (Emmentaler)
250 ml	Sour cream
1 pinch	Nutmeg

Preparation

Total time about 40 minutes

Sift the flour into a bowl and add the egg. Spread the butter in pieces and knead everything well with the salt. Alternatively, use a finished puff pastry! Line a springform pan with the dough.

Cut the ham into cubes and spread it over the dough. Mix the cheese with egg yolk and flour in a bowl. Add sour cream, salt and nutmeg and mix everything well. Beat the egg whites until stiff and fold in.

Spread the cheese mixture on the ham and bake the flan at 200 ° C in the preheated oven for about 30 minutes.

Special tip

Best served with green salad for a full meal!

SAVOY CASSEROLE SWISS TYPE

Ingredients for 4 portions

40 g	Bacon, in strips
40 g	Butter
40 g	Onion
800 g	Savoy cabbage, in strips
Salt and pepper	
200 ml	Vegetable broth
200 ml	Whipped cream
4	Egg
400 g	Emmental cheese, grated
Nutmeg, grated	
Butter for the mold	

Preparation

Total time about 1 hour 10 minutes

Leave out the bacon strips in butter. Braise the onion rings and Savoy cabbage. Salt, pepper, deglaze with vegetable stock and let cook for about 10 minutes.

Mix the cream with the eggs and Emmental cheese, season with salt, pepper and nutmeg.

Fill the steamed savoy cabbage strips into a buttered baking dish, pour the cream and egg mixture over them and put them on the wire rack in the preheated oven. Bake at 180 ° C for about 45 minutes.

CHURER MEAT CAKE

Ingredients for 4 portions

500 g	Minced meat
100 g	Bacon, diced
1	Onion
1	Egg
2 teaspoon	Flour
1 teaspoon	Parsley, chopped
Spice	
1 pack	Puff pastry, rolled out
1	Egg, for brushing

Preparation

Total time about 50 minutes

Mix all the ingredients well into a mixture in a bowl. Put the dough in a springform pan and fill in the mass. Insert edge and cover well. Brush with egg and prick with a fork.

Bake: in the preheated oven, lower groove approx. 40-50 min. A salad is the best match.

BERNER SAUSAGE

Ingredients for 2 portions

2 pairs	Sausages, frankfurters
12 disc	Bacon
150 g	Cheese, (Gouda)
Oil	

Preparation

Total time about 30 minutes

Cut the sausages lengthways so that they remain closed at the ends approx. 2 cm. Cut the cheese into four strips and fill the sausages with it. Wrap strips of bacon around the sausages and fix them with toothpicks.

Heat a little oil in a pan and slowly fry the sausages, turning them over and over.

Serve with fries and salad.

SALMON SNAILS

Ingredients for 6 portions

500 g	Puff pastry, rolled out
250 g	Cream cheese
400 g	Smoked salmon
1 glass	Horseradish

Preparation

Total time about 40 minutes

Spread the cream cheese on the rolled out puff pastry, top with salmon and spread the horseradish paste on it. Roll up well and cut about 2 cm thick slices. Bake in the oven at 180 ° for 25-30 minutes.

BARLEY SOUP ("Gerstensuppe")

Ingredients for 10 portions

25 g	Oil
300 g	Bacon, diced
100 g	Barley
200 g	Onion
300 g	Carrot
200 g	Celery
200 g	Leek
2½ liters	Water
40 g	Broth (instant)
200 g	Cream
50 g	Flour

Salt and pepper, 1 Bay leaf

Preparation

Total time about 2 hour

Heat the oil, add the bacon cubes, fry, add the barley and steam. Only now add the chopped vegetables and also steam them, Season with salt, pepper, bay leaf. Cook with the water and the instant broth for a good 1-2 hours.

Mix the flour and cream only 20 minutes before serving, add to the soup and bring to the boil again.

TURKEY WITH CALVADOS APPLES STUFFING

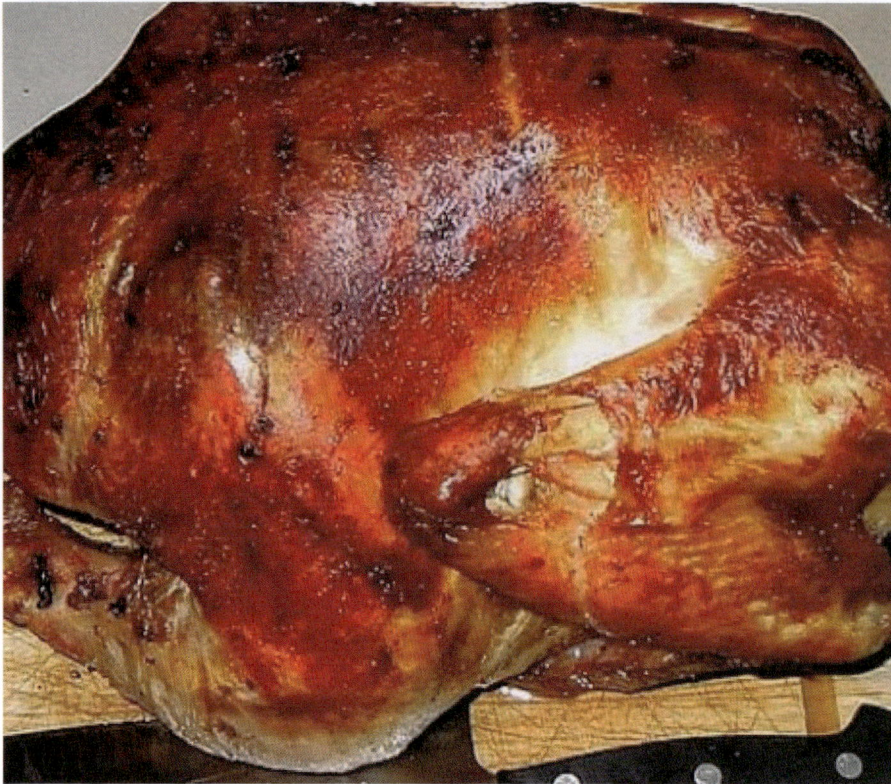

Ingredients for 8 portions

140 g	Apple rings, dried
5 teaspoon	Potato's (boiling), cooked
150 g	Bacon, diced
2	Onion, finely chopped
1 bunch	Parsley, finely chopped
3 teaspoon	Creme fraiche Cheese
1 teaspoon	Salt
Little	Pepper from the grinder
Little	Nutmeg
1	Turkey

Preparation

Total time about 30 minutes

The filling is enough for a 4 kg turkey.

Marinate apple rings with calvados for approx. 3 hours, set aside half, roughly chop the remaining apple rings, put them in a bowl, add the potato cubes and the remaining ingredients up to and including crème fraîche, mix, season.

Filling: Put the filling in the belly. Close the opening with a wooden skewer (or sew it). Salt the turkey. Tie the thighs and wings with kitchen twine, place them on a tray with the breast side up, and pour 50 g of fried butter over them.

You could leave the turkey with the following marinade 3 hours before filling:

1 tbsp mustard, 1 tbsp lemon juice, 4 tbsp peanut oil, 2 tbsp calvados, a little pepper

Mix all the ingredients together, season. Brush the inside and outside of the turkey, cover and marinate in the fridge for 3 hours.

Roast the turkey in the lower half of the oven preheated to 180 ° C for 1 hour. Reduce the heat to 130 ° C, pour 2 dl calvados over the turkey, and continue frying for 2 hours.

Place the apple rings aside, fry for about 1 hour. Occasionally pour the roasting liquid over it. Remove the turkey, cover and leave to rest for about 20 minutes before carving. Pour the frying liquid into a small pan, bring to the boil and serve with the turkey.

Cooking test: prick with a needle, when clear liquid emerges, the turkey is cooked. The core temperature of the turkey should be around 80 ° C.

HORNS WITH CHOPPED APPLESAUCE ("Gehacktes und Hörnli")

Ingredients for 4 portions

700 g	Beef minced meat
3 teaspoon	Butter, for frying
3	Onion, finely chopped
1	Clove of garlic, (pressed)
8 sheets	Sage, (chopped)
3½ dl	Wine, red
1 dl	Meat broth, strong
2 teaspoon	Tomato puree
1 bunch	Parsley, flat-leaved, finely chopped
Salt	
Pepper, black	

| 500 g | Noodles, (croissant noodles) |

Applesauce

Preparation

Total time about 30 minutes

Fry the ground beef in hot fried butter, stirring occasionally, until it is crumbly and almost cooked through. Add onions, garlic and sage and fry briefly. Deglaze with red wine and broth. Add the tomato puree and cook over medium heat for about 20 minutes. Add parsley and season well with salt and pepper. Keep warm until ready to serve.

Cook the croissant noodles in boiling salted water according to the package instructions "al dente". Drain, drain well, mix with liquid butter and serve in deep plates. Spread the minced meat sauce on top and serve with apple sauce.

SWISS ALPINE MACARONS ("Älplermaggronen")

Ingredients for 2 portions

4	Potato
200 g	Macaroni
1	Onion
150 g	Bacon cubes
200 g	Cheese, grated
250 ml	Cream
Salt and pepper	
Nutmeg	

Preparation

Total time about 50 minutes

Peel and dice the potatoes and cook together with the pasta. Possibly add the pasta to the boiling water a few minutes later.

In the meantime, cut the onions into strips and fry them together with the bacon cubes. Drain the potatoes and pasta and mix with the onions and the bacon cubes. Fill this mixture in layers with the cheese in a gratin dish, season the cream with a little pepper and nutmeg and pour over it. Bake in the oven at 150 ° C for about 10 minutes until the cheese has melted.

Mix briefly again at the table. Salad also fits.

MEAT SOUP

Ingredients for 6 portions

2 liters	Water, cold
2	Marrow bone
1	Onion, unpeeled, cutlery (with cloves)
1 toe	Garlic
1 teaspoon	Salt
600 g	Beef, (boiled meat)
600 g	Vegetables, (carrots, celery, leek, cabbage)
4 teaspoon	Parsley, chopped smooth

Preparation

Total time about 1hour 25 minutes

Put cold water in a high pan.

Add the onion, the clove of garlic and the vegetables cut into large pieces and bring to the boil slowly. Season with salt and add meat (the whole piece).

Cover and cook lightly on a low heat.

Rinse the marrow bone for approx. 1 hours and cook for the last 10 minutes.

Before serving, cut the meat into small pieces across the grain and return to the soup.

Sprinkle the chopped parsley on top.

ZUCCHINI CARPACCIO

Ingredients for 4 portions

150 g	Zucchini, sliced into fine slices
1 teaspoon	Soy sauce
1 teaspoon	Apple Cider Vinegar
1 teaspoon	Balsamic
1 Msp	Mustard
4 teaspoon	Olive oil
1 Msp	Lemon peel, grated
1	Tomatoe
½ bunch	Basil
1 teaspoon	Pine nuts

Preparation

Total time about 1 hour 20 minutes

Arrange zucchini on a plate. Prepare a dressing from soy sauce, vinegar, mustard, oil and lemon zest and drizzle over it. Dice the tomato, cut the basil into strips and sprinkle with the pine nuts. Let the sauce soak in, serve.

MEATLOAF ("Hackbraten")

Ingredients for 2 portions

250 g	Ground beef
250 g	Minced pork
100 g	Veal sausage
2 disc	Bread, soaked
1	Egg
2	Onion
2 toes	Garlic, finely chopped or pressed
Salt and pepper	
Thyme	
Rosemary	
N.B	Broth
N.B	Carrot

Preparation

Total time about 1 hour 30 minutes

Mix all the ingredients (meat to rosemary), season and shape into a roast. Sear it briefly on all sides and cook in the oven for about 1 hour at 180 degrees in a broth with carrots and onions. Turn 1-2 times and pour broth over it.

ROAST PORK TICINO STYLE

Ingredients for 4 portions

1	Garlic cloves
1 Msp	Sage
1 Msp	Clove powder
1 teaspoon	Rosemary
1 teaspoon	Lemon zest, grated
1 teaspoon	Oregano
1 teaspoon	Thyme
Salt and pepper	
3 teaspoon	Olive oil
1 kg	Roast pork
125 ml	White wine
½ tsp	Caraway powder

1 teaspoon	Sour cream
Possibly	Starch to bind
N.B	Water

Preparation

Total time about 12 hours 30 minutes

Peel the clove of garlic and chop finely. Finely chop the herbs. Mix both with the other spices and the olive oil to a paste. Rub the meat with it and let it steep overnight.

The next day, fry on all sides in a hot pot, pouring in some water.

Then fry in the preheated oven at 200 ° C (just under) for about 2 1/2 hours. Turn the meat every 15 minutes and always add water in time. At the end of the roasting time, dissolve the roast with white wine, season with caraway powder, salt and pepper. Possibly bind with cornstarch (**but mixed with cold water**). Now pour sour cream into a cup and add some of the hot sauce. Mix well and then stir into the rest of the sauce (this prevents the sour cream from flocculating).

HORN SALAD ("Hörnlisalat")

Ingredients for 8 portions

6 cup	Hörnli (pasta)
1	Bell pepper, red
6	Pickled gherkin
200 g	Cheese, Swiss Emmental cheese
100 g	Ham, or salami
15	Onion (silver onions)
3	Egg
3 teaspoon	Mayonnaise
1 teaspoon	Mustard, mild
1 teaspoon	Aromat, (Swiss spice)
2	Onion
2 toes	Garlic

| 2 teaspoon | Natural yoghurt |

| 1 splash | Tabasco, red |

Parsley, fresh and chives

Paprika powder, salad spice

Vinegar (herbal vinegar)

Olive oil

Curry

Preparation

Total time about 30 minutes

Cook the horns as usual and cool them with cold water.

Cut the bell peppers, pickled cucumbers, Emmental cheese, ham and silver onions into small cubes and place in a large bowl.

Boil the eggs hard, peel and cut them into small pieces and put them in the bowl.

Mix the mayonnaise, mustard, spices and herbs, tabasco, natural yoghurt, vinegar and oil together as usual to the salad dressing. Chop the onions and garlic and add to the sauce.

CAPUNS

Ingredients for 4 portions

250 g	Flour
15 sheets	Swiss chard
3	Egg
2 dl	Milk
1 teaspoon	Salt
1	Sausage, dry sausage like land hunters
60 g	Meat (Bündnerfleisch)
60 g	Ham, raw
1 teaspoon	Parsley
Pepper, freshly ground	
25 g	Butter
1	Onion
½ dl	Broth
30 g	Mountain cheese, grated

| 60 g | Butter |
| 50 g | Bacon, diced |

Preparation

Total time about 35 minutes

Mix the eggs, add 1 dl milk and make the dough with the flour. Cut the meat into cubes, steam the finely chopped onion in butter and add to the batter with the chopped parsley, season with pepper and salt as desired.

Blanch the chard leaves in plenty of water, drain, cut away the leaf ribs. Cover the leaves with stuffing and roll them up.

Steam the capuns in a flat pan with a little butter, add the milk and stock simmer on a small fire for 15 minutes, then drain and serve on a warm plate.

Fry the bacon cubes in a little butter and pour over the capuns, sprinkle with the grated cheese.

DESSERTS

HAZELNUT CHESTNUT CAKE

Ingredients for 1 small cake

70 g	Margarine or butter
2	Egg
70 g	Sugar, brown
1 point	Vanilla sugar
100 g	Hazelnuts, grated
70 g	Chestnut puree, sweet
40 g	Chocolate, bittersweet, finely grated
2 teaspoon	Flour (spelled flour or white flour)
1 tsp.	Baking powder
1 teaspoon	Powdered sugar, for dusting
½ teaspoon	Vanilla sugar, for dusting

Preparation

Total time about 20 minutes

The amount is enough for an 18 springform pan, double for a 26 springform pan and bake for about 10 minutes longer. Stir in the margarine until soft add the eggs, sugar and vanilla sugar, stir

Until frothy, mix in the hazelnuts and chestnut puree, stir in the flour and baking powder, mix the fine grated chocolate with the wooden spoon into the batter.

Bake at 170 ° for approx. 45 minutes.

When the cake has cooled, dust with the mixture of powdered sugar and vanilla sugar.

SWISS PLUM TART ("Zwetschgenwähe")

Ingredients for 2 portions

200 g	Flour
80 g	Butter
1 dl	Water
1 pinch	Salt

For covering:

4	Ladyfingers
500 g	Plums

For the cast:

2 dl	Milk
1 dl	Whipped cream
2 teaspoon	Flour (or cornstarch)
2	Egg
50 g	Powdered sugar
1 pack	Vanilla sugar

Preparation

Total time about 30 minutes

Crumble the butter and flour together, process with the salt water to a dough (sometimes less water than 1 dl is enough, so do not add all the water!). Roll out this dough about 3 mm thin and place it on a buttered tray or the buttered tart pan.

In a multi-grinder, finely grate the ladyfingers and spread the crumbs on the dough. Now halve the plums, remove the stones and spread them with the cut surface upwards on the dough, working from the edge towards the middle.

Mix all the ingredients for the pour well together, preferably with a hand blender, and pour the pouring onto the flan.

Bake in hot air at 170 ° for 40 - 45 minutes.

The flan tastes best lukewarm. You can also cover them with fresh apricots.

SWISS TOBLERONE MOUSSE CAKE

Ingredients for 1 cake

300 g	Chocolate (Toblerone, whole milk)
2	Egg
4 dl	Whipped cream
1 pack	Cream stiff
2 sheets	Gelatine
1	Cake base, dark, cut twice

Preparation

Total time about 4 hours 30 minutes

Soak the gelatin in cold water. Put water in a pan and put a small bowl in the hot water. Break the brown chocolate into pieces and let it melt in the bowl.

In addition, stir 2 eggs until frothy. Whip 4 dl of whipped cream with 1 pound of cream stiff. Stir 2 squeezed gelatine leaves very quickly in the warm (**but not hot**) chocolate mixture and add the eggs.

Warning, the chocolate clumps very quickly. This is why fast work is required in this step! Mix everything immediately with the mixer so that the mass becomes supple again. Fold in the cream.

Repeat everything with white Toblerone

Place the sponge cake in a 26 springform pan. Spread 2/3 of the brown mousse on the sponge cake base. Place the middle bottom on the cream. Spread white mousse on top. Put the last biscuit part on top and spread the rest of the brown mousse on nicely. Let it harden in the fridge (approx. 4 h)

GINGERBREAD ("Lebkuchen")

Ingredients for 1 cake

500 g	Flour
500 g	Sugar
3 teaspoon	Cocoa powder
3 teaspoon	Ginger bread spice
1 pack	Baking powder
5 dl	Milk
4 teaspoon	Oil

Preparation

Total time about 55 minutes

Sift the flour into a bowl. Add sugar, cocoa powder, gingerbread spice and the baking powder. Gradually pour the milk and oil into the well, stir in and stir until smooth.

Empty the dough into the baking sheet covered with baking paper.

Baking: Do not preheat the oven and slide the tray into the middle groove. Bake on good medium heat (180 ° C) for 30 - 40 minutes.

Note: Cut the cooled gingerbread into pieces of any size. This gingerbread tastes excellent with black tea or milk coffee. As a fine addition: spread a little butter on the pieces of gingerbread.

MARZIPAN PLUM CAKE ("Zwetschgenkuchen mit Marzipan")

Ingredients for 2 portions

1 kg	Plum, red or blue
125 g	Butter or margarine
125 g	Sugar
100 g	Raw marzipan
3	Egg
½ bottle	Bitter almond flavor
4 teaspoon	Milk
250 g	Flour
½ point	Baking powder
2 teaspoon	Powdered sugar for sprinkling

Preparation

Total time about 1 hour 45 minutes

Wash the plums, pat them dry, remove the stones and quarter them.

For the batter, stir in the fat and sugar until frothy. Cut marzipan into small pieces, add and stir until smooth. Stir in the eggs one at a time. Mix in the baking aroma and milk. Mix the flour and baking powder and gradually stir in as well. Fill the dough into a greased springform pan (**26 cm in diameter**). Put the prepared plums tightly into the dough.

Bake the cake in the preheated oven at 175 ° C for about 60 to 70 minutes. If necessary, cover with parchment paper after approx. 40 minutes of baking time.

Let the cake cool and dust with icing sugar.

Tip: The cake tastes even better if you stir 2 tablespoons of Amaretto into the dough instead of the baking aroma.

MISSISSIPPI CAKE

Ingredients for 1 cake

50 ml	Water
2 teaspoon	Coffee powder, instant (Nescafe)
175 g	Margarine, soft
100 ml	Cream
4	Egg
275 g	Sugar
1 teaspoon	Vanilla sugar
1 pinch	Salt
100 g	Cocoa powder (chocolate powder)
250 g	Flour
1 teaspoon	Baking powder

Preparation

Total time about 20 minutes

Dissolve the coffee powder in water and put it in a mixing bowl. Add margarine, cream and eggs and mix with a blender. Add sugar, vanilla sugar and salt and stir. Stir in the cocoa powder, then add the flour and baking powder and stir until smooth dough is formed. Fill a prepared 30 cm box mold with 1/3 of the dough and place 2 chocolate bars lengthways on the dough. Pour in 1/3 dough again and insert 2 chocolate bars again. Pour in the rest of the dough and put the 2 last chocolate bars on top.

Special tip:

Children adore this one!

AARGAUER CARROT CAKE ("Aargauer Rüeblikuchen")

Ingredients for 1 cake

250 g	Carrot, finely grated
5	Eggs, separated
175 g	Sugar
1 pinch	Cinnamon
1 pinch	Salt
250 g	Almond, ground
100 g	Flour
1 teaspoon	Baking powder
200 g	Icing sugar
12	Marzipan - Rüebli as decoration
2 teaspoon	Water or lemon juice

Preparation

Total time about 25 minutes, baking 60 minutes

Beat the egg yolk with the sugar until fluffy. Beat egg whites to very stiff snow. Mix the flour, almonds, baking powder, cinnamon and salt. Gradually add the flour mixture and egg whites under the egg yolk mixture. Finally, add the grated carrots. Pour the mixture into a greased springform pan (26 cm) and bake immediately in the preheated oven at 175 ° C for about 60 minutes.

For the icing, mix the icing sugar with 1-2 tablespoons of liquid water or also lemon / orange juice. Brush the cooled cake with it and decorate with the marzipan carrots. The beet cake remains fresh for a few days, so it can be prepared very well.

Instead of the icing, the turnip cake can only be spread with whipped cream.

Instead of the Rüebli, grated apples also taste delicious.

Variant: CARROT CAKE WITHOUT FLOUR ("Rüeblikuchen")

Ingredients for 1 cake

300 g	Carrot
5	Eggs
200 g	Sugar
250 g	Hazelnuts, grated
80 g	Breadcrumbs
½ teaspoon	Baking powder
½ teaspoon	Cinnamon
1 teaspoon	Rum
150 g	Powdered sugar
2 teaspoon	Lemon juice

Preparation

Total time about 1 hour 20 minutes

Peel and grate the carrots.

Separate the eggs and stir the egg yolk with 5 tablespoons of water and the sugar until it is foamy. Beat the egg whites until stiff and add to the egg yolk mixture, add the carrots, hazelnuts, breadcrumbs, baking powder, cinnamon and rum and carefully fold everything in. Bake in a greased pan with breadcrumbs at 180 degrees for 60 minutes.

For the icing, mix the icing sugar with the lemon juice and cover the cooled cake with it. It works a bit at the beginning, but it becomes solid when it is dry.

The cake tastes really good the next day and can be saved for several days.

SWISS APPLE PIE

Ingredients for 1 pie

125 g	Butter
4 m. In size	Egg
75 g	Sugar
150 g	Flour
¼ teaspoon	Baking powder
600 g	Apples, sour
1 large	Lemon juice from the bottle
125 g	Butter, soft
50 g	Powdered sugar
1 teaspoon	Custard powder

Preparation

Total time about 1 hour 30 minutes

Preheat the oven to 175 ° C top / bottom heat (gas: level 2). Grease a springform pan.

Melt the butter, let cool slightly. Mix the eggs and sugar until creamy. Mix the flour with the baking powder and quickly fold into the egg cream. Stir in the melted butter. Spread the dough into the pan, forming a 4 cm high rim. Cool the dough in the tin.

Squeeze the lemon. Wash, peel and quarter apples and remove the core. Cut or slice the apple quarters lengthways and sprinkle with the lemon juice so that they do not turn brown.

Mix the butter with powdered sugar and pudding powder until creamy. Separate the eggs. Stir the egg yolks into the butter mixture. Beat the egg whites until stiff and fold in the egg whites. Mix the apple slices with the cream and fill this into the prepared form with the batter.

Bake the cake in the oven for about 55 minutes. If it browns too much, cover it with aluminum foil. Allow to cool in the mold. Dust with 30 g of powdered sugar before serving.

PEANUT BUTTER COOKIES

Ingredients for 1 portion

1 ¼ cup	Flour
¾ TL	Baking soda
¼ tsp	Salt
½ cup	Butter or margarine
½ cup	Peanut butter
½ cup	Sugar
½ cup	Cane sugar
1	Egg
½	Vanilla bean, scratched out marrow

Preparation

Total time about 20 minutes

Preheat the oven to 190 ° C.

Mix flour with baking soda and salt. Stir the butter or margarine until small peaks form. Add the peanut butter, sugar and raw sugar and stir again very well. Now add the egg and the vanilla pulp and stir everything vigorously again. Add the flour mixture and knead everything until it is compact dough.

Form small balls out of the dough, roll them (if desired) in sugar and place them on a baking sheet lined with baking paper. Use a fork to gently flatten the beads.

Bake for about 10 minutes. Leave the beads on the hot tray for about 1 minute before placing them on a cooling rack.

SWISS NUT THALER

Ingredients for 4 portions

125 g	Hazelnuts
250 g	Flour
1 teaspoon	Baking powder
100 g	Food starch
100 g	Powdered sugar
1 pack	Vanilla sugar
1 pinch	Salt
250 g	Butter
	Cocoa powder

Preparation

Total time about 12 hours 30 minutes

Quickly knead nuts, flour, baking powder, corn-starch, powdered sugar, vanilla sugar, salt and butter into a dough, form four rolls of about three centimetres in diameter. Roll in cocoa powder until the rolls are evenly brown on the outside and chill overnight.

The next day, cut into ½ cm slices with a knife and bake at 180 ° on the middle shelf in 15 to 20 minutes light yellow. Attention, the thaler will turn brown too easily!

The cookies have to stand in a tightly closed tin for a few days, only then will they taste really good.

RAISIN CAKES

Ingredients for 1 portion

100 g	Raisins
50 g	Butter, soft
50 g	Sugar
1	Egg
1	Lemon, grated zest of it
150 g	Flour

Preparation

Total time about 20 minutes

Use a trowel to stir the butter until small peaks form. Mix in sugar, egg and lemon zest one after the other. Mix the flour and the raisins well and add gradually.

Cut off small piles from the dough with 2 teaspoons and place on a baking sheet covered with baking paper. Approx. bake for 15 minutes in an oven preheated to 200 ° C until golden brown.

If you like, you can make a glaze from 50 g of powdered sugar and 1 tablespoon of lemon juice and spread it on the warm biscuits. But they also taste delicious without them.

THURGAU MOST CREAM ("Thurgauer Mostcreme")

1

Ingredients for 10 portions

1 liter	Apple juice
120 g	Sugar
2	Egg
50 g	Cornstarch
2 dl	Cream
Possibly	Calvados

Preparation

Total time about 15 minutes

Mix the sugar and eggs in a bowl until creamy.

Dissolve the corn-starch in a large pan with approx. 1dl of the apple juice. Add the rest of the apple juice and the egg and sugar mixture and bring to the boil while stirring constantly. Then let it cool completely (this can be prepared up to two days in advance).

Before serving, whip the cream until stiff and carefully pull it under the cold cream.

Decorate with dried or fresh apple rings and serve.

Hint: "Most" means apple juice.

BLACK CHOCOLATE MOUSSE

Ingredients for 4 portions

300 g	Chocolate, bittersweet
45 g	Butter
2 cl	Rum
6	Eggs

Preparation

Total time about 30 minutes (+ refrigerate for about 4 hours)

Separate eggs, whip egg whites until stiff.

Melt chocolate and butter in a water bath, gradually add egg yolk. Carefully fold in the rum and beaten egg whites. Refrigerate.

CHOCOLATE CREAM ROLL

Ingredients for 2 portions

4	Protein
4 teaspoon	Water
200 g	Sugar
4	Egg yolk
60 g	Flour
60 g	Corn-starch (Maizena)
½ tsp.	Baking powder
40 g	Cocoa powder, (not sweetened)
¼ liter	Cream
1 pack	Vanilla sugar
Cake icing, chocolate	
50 g	Coconut fat

100 g	Chocolate, bittersweet
50 g	Chocolate, whole milk
Rum	
Possibly	Powdered sugar
Possibly	Jam

Preparation

Total time about 30 minutes

Beat egg white and cold water until stiff. Let the sugar pour in and whisk briefly below. Add the egg yolks.

Mix the flour, corn-starch, baking powder and cocoa, sieve over and fold in loosely.

Line the baking sheet with baking paper and spread the dough on it and bake in the preheated oven at 190 ° for about 15 minutes (middle rail).

Immediately drop the sponge cake onto a cloth and carefully peel off the paper. Include the dough sheet including the cloth and let it cool in the cloth.

Whip the cream with cream stiff, vanilla sugar (possibly also some sugar) well.

Now carefully roll up the cooled dough sheet and drizzle with a little rum. Then spread the whipped cream and roll it in again using the cloth.

You can now pour a chocolate glaze over it and decorate it as desired or just sprinkle with icing sugar.

For the glaze let the coconut fats slowly melts and add the chocolates. (Don't let the fat get hot). When the chocolate has melted, stir everything well and let it cool down a bit. Only shortly before the mass becomes thick, pour the glaze over it. It will be especially beautiful if you brush the roulade with hot jam beforehand!

HAZELNUT STENGELI

Ingredients for 4 portions

100 g	Butter
125 g	Sugar
2	Egg yolk
1 pinch	Salt
125 g	Hazelnuts, grated
150 g	Flour
1	Egg yolk, (for brushing)

Preparation

Total time about 1 hour 30 minutes

Stir butter, sugar and egg yolk until foamy for 10 minutes. Add hazelnuts, salt and flour. Let the dough rest in the cold for 1 hour. Forming

Roll out the dough 1 cm thick. Cut finger-long and finger-wide stems, brush with egg yolk.

Baking: Bake In the middle of the oven preheated to 180 ° (gas level 2) for 20 minutes.

CIGAR DONUT

Ingredients for 3 portions

500 g	Puff pastry
150 g	Quark (Ziger), can be replaced by low-fat curd or ricotta
½ tsp	Cinnamon
30 g	Raisins, washed
100 g	Almond, ground
1 teaspoon	Lemon zest, grated
80 g	Sugar
Oil, for deep frying	
4 tbsp	Sugar, for sprinkling
1 teaspoon	Cinnamon, for sprinkling

Preparation

Total time about 30 minutes

Roll out the puff pastry about 2 mm thick and cut out squares with a side length of 10 cm. Mix the cigars, cinnamon, raisins, almonds, lemon zest and sugar into a moist but not liquid mixture (if it seems too dry, stir in a little cream). Put 1 tablespoon of filling on each dough square brush the edges of the dough with a little water and roll the dough diagonally so that triangular donuts are formed. Press the edges firmly together.

Heat the oil to 170 degrees and fry the donuts in portions in the hot oil until they are golden yellow. Mix the cinnamon and sugar and turn the hot donuts inside.

CRANBERRY CAKE

Ingredients for 2 portions

150 g	Butter or margarine
200 g	Sugar
1 teaspoon	Cardamom
1 pinch	Salt
3	Egg
150 g	Nuts (pecan nuts) or almonds, roughly chopped
250 g	Flour
2 Teaspoons	Baking powder
340 g	Berries (cranberry)

Preparation

Total time about 1 hour 20 minutes

Stir butter in a bowl until soft. Add sugar, cardamom and salt. Mix in one egg at a time keep stirring until the mixture is light.

Mix in the nuts. Mix the flour and baking powder and stir into the mixture.

Carefully fold the cranberries under the mixture, fill the batter into a greased and floured (or lined with baking paper) form approx. 30 cm long.

Bake in the oven preheated to 180 ° C for approx. 1 hour.

HASLI CAKE

Ingredients for 3 portions

500 g	Choice of dough (cake batter)
150 g	Ground hazelnuts
150 g	Hazelnuts, chopped
200 g	Sugar
1 teaspoon	cinnamon
1 pinch	Salt
3	Egg
1 dl	Cream
1 dl	Milk
1 teaspoon	Flour

Powdered sugar for sprinkling

Preparation

Total time about 50 minutes

Roll out the dough for a round baking sheet (diameter 28 cm). Grease the sheet, cover and prick the cake batter.

Mix all other ingredients into a viscous dough and spread over the cake batter. Bake in a hot oven at 180 ° C for about 30 minutes.

Make a paper cut of your choice from a paper, place on the finished cake and sprinkle with the powdered sugar.

BASLER TREATS ("Basler Läckerli")

Ingredients for 3 portions

450 g	Honey
300 g	Sugar
½ tbsp	Cinnamon
1 pinch	Clove powder
½ tsp	Nutmeg
100 g	Orange peel, chopped
100 g	Lemon, chopped
200 g	Almond, roughly chopped
1	organic, grated zest
100 ml	Cherry water
600 g	Flour
½ tsp	Baking powder

| 150 g | Powdered sugar |
| 3 teaspoon | Water |

Preparation

Total time about 8 hours 30 minutes

Slowly bring the honey, sugar and spices to a boil in a saucepan and remove from the fire. Add the orange peel, lemon, almonds and grated lemon peel and mix everything. Add cherry water, flour and baking powder and mix everything into dough.

Roll out the still warm dough, approx. 5 mm thick, on two sheet metal backs sprinkled with flour and let it rest for a few hours (e.g. overnight). Then bake in the middle of the preheated oven for 15 to 20 minutes at 190 degrees (forced air).

Mix icing sugar with water for the glaze, immediately glaze after baking, cut off the hard edge and then cut the treats into pieces measuring approx. 4 cm by 5 cm with a pizza roller (or carefully with a knife).

The treats are best kept in a plastic bag. They should not dry out completely otherwise they can become very hard. They taste good all year round and go well with a good glass of red wine!

STOMACH BREAD ("Magenbrot")

Ingredients for 10 portions

500 g	Flour (smoked flour)
1 teaspoon	Baking powder
2 teaspoon	Cocoa powder
2 pinches	Salt
2 pinches	Nutmeg
450 g	Sugar
1½ dl	Milk
1½ dl	Water
1 teaspoon	Cherry water
200 g	Chocolate, dark

40 g	Butter
500 g	Powdered sugar
4 pinches	Cinnamon
3pinches	Carnation, ground
2 pinches	nutmeg

Preparation

Total time about 1 hour 45 minutes

Mix the flour and all the ingredients up to and including nutmeg in a bowl.

Add sugar, milk, water and cherry, knead into smooth dough. Place the dough on a sheet of baking paper, spread out to a rectangle of approx. 25x30 cm. (Tip: spread out the dough with a wet spatula)

Baking approx 20 minutes in the lower half of the oven which has been preheated to 180 degrees, take out, cool slightly, drop onto a grill remove paper, cool. Cut into pieces approx. 2x4 cm, put in a large bowl.

Glaze: Melt the chocolate with butter and water in a small pan over low heat remove the pan from the plate.

Add powdered sugar and spices, stir until smooth. Pour the glaze over the pieces, mix until all are evenly coated. Place on a grid, dry for approx. 1 hour.

EGGNOG PIE

Ingredients for 16 portions

100 g	Chocolate, bittersweet
5	Egg
80 g	Butter or margarine
100 g	Sugar
1 pack	Taste of rum
8 teaspoon	Eggnog, (or a little more)
200 g	Almond, ground
400 g	Whipped cream
2 pack	Vanilla sugar
1 pack	Creamy
75 g	Grated chocolate

Preparation

Total time about 45 minutes

Chop the chocolate and separate the eggs.

Beat the egg yolk, fat and sugar until creamy with the whisk on the hand mixer. Add rum back, 2 tablespoons of eggnog, almonds and chopped chocolate and mix in. Beat the egg whites until stiff and carefully fold them under the dough.

Line a springform pan (diameter 24 cm) with baking paper and fill in the dough. Bake in the preheated oven (electric cooker: 200 ° C, gas cooker: setting 3) for 25 to 30 minutes. Remove the cake from the tin and let it cool.

Whip the cream, vanilla sugar and cream fixer until stiff. Pour a quarter of the cream into a piping bag with a star nozzle. Spread the remaining cream evenly on the cake top and edge. Decorate the cake with cream dots from a piping bag and sprinkle the grated chocolate on the edge and the cream dots. Finally pour the remaining egg liqueur into the middle of the cake and let it run carefully.

MORE ENGLISH BOOKS
FROM LACHLAN ANDERSON

Coorie Cooking: Scottish Recipes To Warm Your Heart And Heal Your Soul

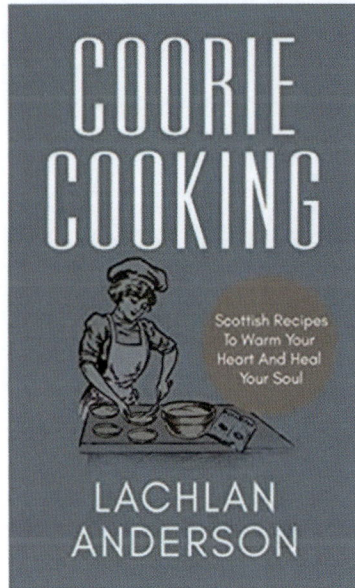

50 easy recipes for cooking with beer

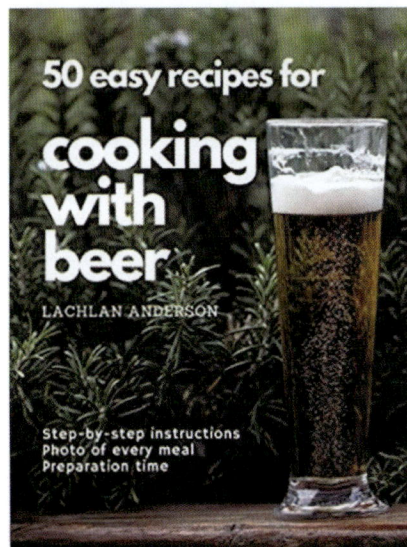

Coorie: What You Need to Know About The Scottish Lifestyle Trend

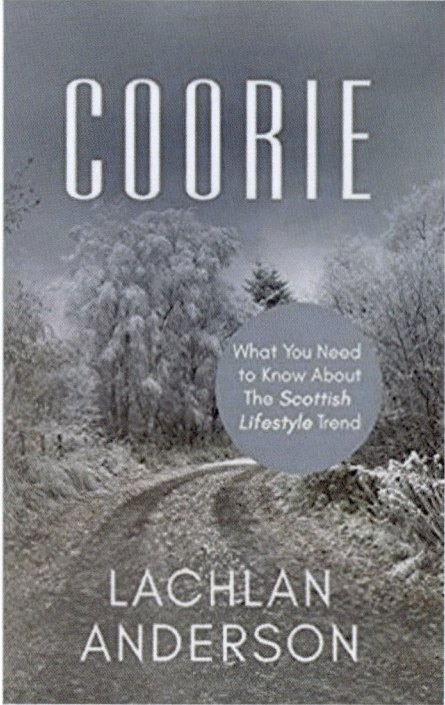

The Coorie Adult Coloring Book

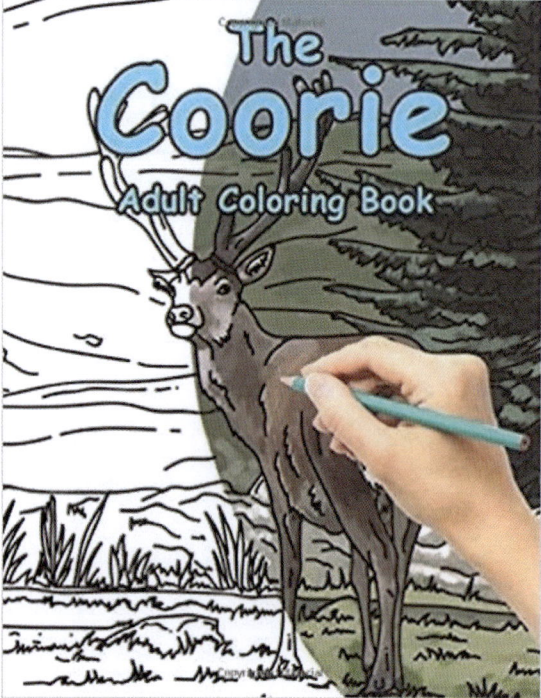

Cooking With Friends: Coloring Book For Kids

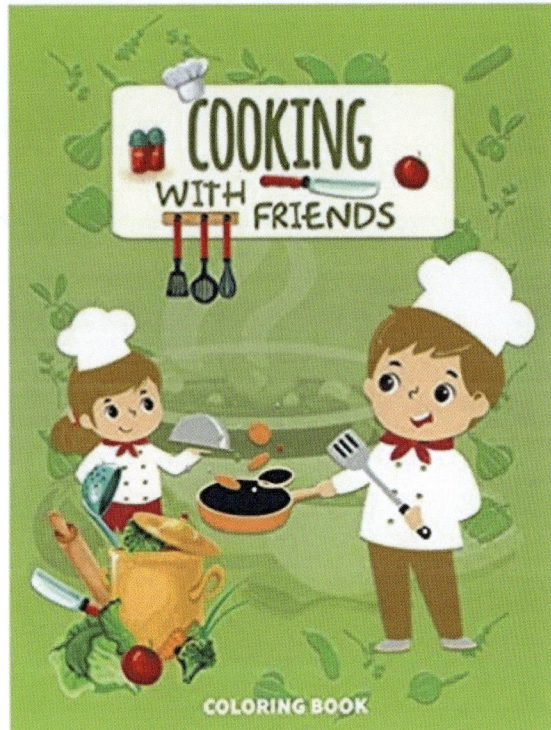

DEUTSCHE BÜCHER
VON LACHLAN ANDERSON

Coorie Cooking - Schottische Rezepte zum Wohlfühlen: Schottlands Küche mit Coorie Rezepten (mit Farbfotos)

Coorie: Was Sie über den schottischen Lifestyle-Trend wissen müssen

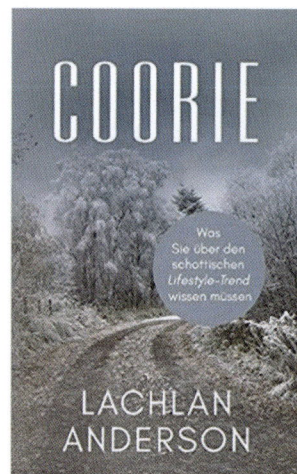

TO FINISH...

I hope you enjoyed these recipes and had a great lunch or dinner with some of them! Thank you for buying this book and trusting my cooking.

I have invested a lot of evenings in putting together all these recipes and creating this great book. If you did me the favour of writing a short review on amazon or wherever you bought the book and have access to review it, this would make me extremely happy! Readers often underestimate the value their reviews have. In addition, as for me, I read every review, as it helps me to write better books in the future.

So thank you very much and ... enjoy your meal!

Printed in Great Britain
by Amazon